10 THINGS
YOU SHOULD KNOW ABOUT
MARRIAGE

AJMAL MASROOR

Barefoot Institute

Barefoot Institute
15 Pellatt Grove
London N22 5NP
00 44 (0)5602 447 022
www.barefootinstitute.com

First publishes in Great Britain in 2010

Published by Barefoot Institute
© Barefoot Institute 2010

The right of Ajmal Masroor to be identified as author of this work
has been asserted by his accordance with the Copyright, Designs
and Patents Act 1988

ISBN: 978-0-9567246-0-1

هُنَّ لِبَاسٌ لَّكُمْ وَأَنتُمْ لِبَاسٌ لَّهُنَّ

They are your garments and ye are their garments
(Quran 2:187)

Contents

Foreword

The garment metaphor of the Qur'an however offers us an opportunity to redress the current gender disequilibrium and disease. Garments protect us from the perils of the elements, they hide our faults, and they beautify us. Such a metaphor if applied to our daily lives would enable men and women to not only live more harmoniously together, it would create a more stable framework on which to build our societies. Surely men and women are the corner stone of societies, and the marital relationship has the potential to be the very foundation of community and social advancement.

Yet if this relationship is unbalanced, corrosive, or lacks harmony, then the potential benefits and social empowerment of both genders united in common endeavour cannot be realised. Instead, rising divorce rates, serial monogamy, infidelity, and a general lack of cooperation will eat at the heart of the sacred union of marriage, and eat away at the heart of our societies.

All too often marriage seems the end of the journey; the "happy ever after" of the fairy tale, yet marriage is just the beginning of the journey. If those marriages can be based not only on trust, love and mutual respect; but on the Qur'anic notion of garments and protecting friendship, then perhaps we can restore balance to ourselves and to our societies.

Initiatives such as "Ten Things You Should Know About Marriage", inspired by the Qur'anic paradigms, help address some of these issues. Such endeavours to empower people to find solace and contentment in their married life are not only welcome, but vital if we are to make marital success not just an aspiration but a lived reality.

Sarah Joseph OBE
London, 2010

Background

I would like to share with you my story. In fact, it is not just a story, it was one of the biggest challenges in my life and it left me with a huge void and emotional scar.

I was a 25 year old, impressionable young man looking to get married. Through a mutual friend I was introduced to an eligible young woman. We considered each other for marriage, informed our parents and all seemed fine, so we decided to get married. Within the first few weeks of marriage my dream of married life was challenged. As weeks rolled into months and months into years, our marriage went from bad to worse. Constant arguments, resentment, frustration, recrimination and internal strife became part of our everyday life. We drifted away from each other.

I desperately wanted help. I spoke to friends who shied away from supporting us. I spoke to our families they had no idea what to do. I sought help from Muslim scholars and teachers. All to no avail! Eventually, I gave up and walked out. I accepted defeat, swallowed my pride and went for divorce - the ultimate safety button.

I later enrolled with Relate, the relationship counselling agency, to learn about what went wrong with my marriage and to help others. I wanted to help prepare others before they signed the marriage contract. I spent years learning how to counsel couples and it was one of my best experiences. In hindsight, I wish I had known as much about relationships during my troubled marriage as I know now. I would probably still be married to my former wife.

I have never thought of that episode in my life as a failure. I have learnt from it and have taken it to be a great opportunity to mend my old ways, start afresh and, most importantly, help others make sense of what it means to be married. One regret is the fact that during those troubled days nobody was running a marriage preparation course. There were no support facilities for young Muslim couples who are struggling.

That has been the main motivation behind this book. I would like to help people prepare for marriage, make better sense of the complexities of balancing the various aspects of relationships, and feel fully equipped to face the challenges of married life.

This handbook is a small attempt to shed some light on the inner workings of marital life. It is a humble attempt to prompt young people to prepare for marriage adequately. It is also a small token of help for those who are married but struggling.

I would like to dedicate this book to those who are doing everything to build mutual happiness. As far as I am concerned, it is my new wife who has given me some of the best years of my life so far, with her deep love and dedication. She is truly a remarkable woman and I am grateful to her and to Allah for blessing me with her.

> Never be shy in seeking professional help if you are struggling in your marriage, there are people out there who can help you!

يَا أَيُّهَا النَّاسُ اتَّقُواْ رَبَّكُمُ الَّذِي خَلَقَكُم مِّن نَّفْسٍ وَاحِدَةٍ وَخَلَقَ مِنْهَا زَوْجَهَا وَبَثَّ مِنْهُمَا رِجَالاً كَثِيرًا وَنِسَاء وَاتَّقُواْ اللّهَ الَّذِي تَسَاءلُونَ بِهِ وَالأَرْحَامَ إِنَّ اللّهَ كَانَ عَلَيْكُمْ رَقِيبًا

O MANKIND!

Be conscious of your Sustainer, who has created you out of one living entity, and out of it created its mate, and out of the two spread abroad a multitude of men and women. And remain conscious of God, in whose name you demand [your rights] from one another, and of these ties of kinship. Verily, God is ever watchful over you!

(Quran 4:1)

Introduction

> "O young men, those among you who can support a wife should marry, for it restrains the eyes from casting (lustful glances), and preserves one from immorality." *(Hadith Muslim)*

In Islam, marriage is highly recommended as it helps:

- Develop a safe and secure environment to explore and express emotions
- Enjoy mutual intimacy and sexual pleasures
- Creating an environment for bringing up children
- Bring equilibrium and balance physically and emotionally

Marriage in Islam is always between a man and woman who freely and without coercion consent to marriage and are of marriageable age. Many people wonder if marriage in Islam is really an obligation. Marriage is an obligation for those who are:

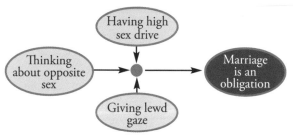

It is an obligation for those who fear that their sexual desires are so overwhelming that they are in imminent danger of having sex outside marriage. It is important to note that people should not get married just to have sex.

There are those who constantly ogle every woman with their lustful gaze. The blessed Prophet advised young Ali: "O Ali Listen! Don't continue with looking (at women), as the first look is [permitted] for you, while the second is not." *(Hadith Tirmidhi)*

So if you find yourself staring at every woman you see you need to stop and start seriously considering marriage.

Conversely, according to Islam, if someone fears that they will be harmful emotionally or physically to their spouse, marriage would be forbidden for them.

Marriage in Islam is a social contract between two consenting adults, male and female, to work together as partners in pursuit of mutual happiness and satisfaction.

Marriage requires commitment and hard work. In our celebrity-obsessed, sound-bite driven and materially-motivated culture, many marriages fail. Amongst many reasons, the key one is selfishness. It is "me, me and me" that many people are addicted to. Marriage is the anti-thesis to this destructive phenomenon.

We all deserve to be loved and to love, to share our life with somebody and find mutual satisfaction. We all deserve to be happy.

An old man once told his grandson, "My son! Marriage is not a state of being but a state of becoming".

Marriage is a journey most people long to embark on. It is the most deeply soul-challenging and testing journey we will ever make. Marriage can bring out the best or the worst in us. Adequate preparation, reflection and commitment, maturity and willingness can immeasurably help it bring out the best.

This book takes you on a journey that I hope will help you can make the best choices for your marriage.

Are you ready?

Please place a tick or cross next to each of the statements that represent your person view about yourself in the table below:

	✗	✓
I am emotionally stable		
I can articulate how I feel		
I can communicate my thoughts to people clearly and openly		
I am happy to be in my own company		
I enjoy spending time with others		
I know what makes me happy		
I know that love is hard work		
I know what I can offer to my partner		
I have done what I wanted to do in life as a single person		
I can solve problems competently and with sensitivity		
I can make independent decisions		
I am able to compromise		
I can negotiate well with others to find a mutually satisfactory solution		
I understand the concept of independence		
I understand the concept of belonging		
I know what is really important to me		
I know how to deal with my negative emotions		
I understand what areas of my life I need to work on or improve		
I am financially stable and secure		

The outcome of the exercise is outlined below. If you have:

- Under 7 ticks: You are not ready for marriage
- 7-14: You are on your way and could do with a marriage training programme
- 14 and over: You are ready for marriage, enjoy the rest of the book

Your score from this exercise is only an indication of your personal state, it is not conclusive, but taking active measures to prepare for marriage will only enable you to enjoy a more fulfilling life with your spouse.

> We all deserve to be loved and to love, to share our life with somebody and find mutual satisfaction. We all deserve to be happy.

هُوَ الَّذِي خَلَقَكُم مِّن نَّفْسٍ وَاحِدَةٍ وَجَعَلَ
مِنْهَا زَوْجَهَا لِيَسْكُنَ إِلَيْهَا فَلَمَّا تَغَشَّاهَا
حَمَلَتْ حَمْلاً خَفِيفًا فَمَرَّتْ بِهِ فَلَمَّا أَثْقَلَت
دَّعَوَا اللَّهَ رَبَّهُمَا لَئِنْ آتَيْتَنَا صَالِحاً لَّنَكُونَنَّ
مِنَ الشَّاكِرِينَ

It is He who has created you [all] out of one living
entity, and out of it brought into being its mate, so
that man might incline [with love] towards woman.
And so, when he has embraced her, she conceives
[what at first is] a light burden, and continues to
bear it. Then, when she grows heavy [with child],
they both call unto God, their Sustainer, "If You
indeed grant us a sound [child], we shall most
certainly be among the grateful!"
(Quran 7:189)

01

Marriage is half of your religion but he/she is not the other half

"When a person marries, he has fulfilled half of his religion, so let him fear Allah regarding the remaining half."
(Hadith Baihaqi)

Many people often misunderstand this Prophetic statement. Some think it literally means half of your religion while others dismiss it as a poetic expression.

One could interpret this hadith (the tradition of the blessed Prophet) in the following ways:
- This is a metaphor to encourage people to get married.
- It is an illustration of how one cannot practice Islam without a family.
- It highlights the mutual role of husband and wife to support and help sustain each other in their spiritual practices and growth.

The common misunderstanding is best described in the following sentiment: "Let me find a pious spouse and s/he will make me pious."

This misconception ruins many relationships. No one will make you pious; you yourself will have to make a conscious effort to change for the better.

The realisation for change must be your own and not because of somebody else. If it is imposed or done to please someone else, it will be short-lived and often fosters resentment.

Marriage is a journey of two people, not a lonely path, with a loving, kind and supporting companion.

You help each other in this journey. You provide a helping hand if your spouse is down, you provide a broad shoulder if your spouse needs support, you provide kindness, love and compassion. It is always mutual.

Together you are:

- Best friends
- Brilliant companions
- Wise advisers
- Loyal spouses
- Intimate partners

In so doing you fulfil your Islamic obligations towards each other. In creating such a safe and secure space you are able to devote more time in seeking the pleasure of Allah. Mutual sexual gratification provides the feeling of purity and frees you to enhance your moral and personal character.

"Marriage is half of your religion" can be understood in all the above mentioned ways. If you are able to eliminate all the threats that prevent you from finding contentment you have won half the battle. Marriage is all about finding, through mutual support, Allah's light in your life.

There are two key ingredients in finding the pleasure of Allah and the pleasure of one's spouse:

- **Clean heart** - Allah's light resides in all our hearts. When we obscure it with sins and arrogance we suffer from all sorts of spiritual ailments. When we keep it clean, it illuminates us and our surrounding. Illnesses of the heart have a profound negative impact on our spouses. Hearts have a unique way of communicating with each other. Keep it healthy and clean and your marriage will be fulfilling for you.

- **Fair dealing** - Being fair and just is closest to being Allah-conscious. Being fair to Allah is about being loyal to Him, following His advice to the best of your ability. "The best person in the eyes of Allah is the one who is fair to his/her spouse", reminded the blessed Prophet *(Hadith Tirmidhi)*. Treat your spouse the way you would like to be treated – fairly.

Tips and tabs

Self-evaluation
Please place a tick in the appropriate column below

	Always	Fairly Regularly	Not regularly	Hardly ever	Never
I am regular with my prayers					
I read Qur'an regularly					
I attend an Islamic study group					
I fast in Ramadan					
I pay Zakah					
I keep good company and friends					
I keep ties with my family (close and extended)					
I do not swear					
I do not have a vulgar tongue					
I am not abusive when I am angry					
I am mindful of Allah - in times of adversity					
I am mindful of Allah - in times of abundance					
I am direct (do not beat around the bush)					
I do not gossip					
I do not lie					
I forgive people easily					
I know how to manage anger					
I am good to my neighbours					
I am prepared to forgive and forget					

Reflection

- How do you evaluate your responses?
- What have you learnt by doing this exercise?
- How does it feel to take a closer look at your personal spiritual state?

Now take a deep breath and think where your personal spiritual state is. Regardless of who you get married to, they will not be able to fulfil even a fraction of your faith let alone half of it. Faith is yours, practicing your faith is also your duty. Your spouse could remind you, but it is your duty, solely your responsibility.

Exercise 1:
Defining marriage – What is your definition of marriage? Write down your thoughts and share it with your spouse or prospective spouse.

Exercise 2:
Reflection on an existing definition – Reflect on the following statement and write down your thoughts. You can share it with your spouse or prospective spouse.

> "Marriage is not a static state between two unchanging people. Marriage is a psychological and spiritual journey that begins in the ecstasy of attraction, meanders through a rocky stretch of self-discovery and culminates in the creation of an intimate, joyful, lifelong union". *(Harville Hendrix)*

Your spiritual and physical fulfilment is entirely your own, no one can do it for you. If you look for a spouse to complete something in you, you may not find it!

وَمِنْ آيَاتِهِ أَنْ خَلَقَ لَكُم مِّنْ أَنفُسِكُمْ
أَزْوَاجًا لِّتَسْكُنُوا إِلَيْهَا وَجَعَلَ بَيْنَكُم
مَّوَدَّةً وَرَحْمَةً إِنَّ فِي ذَلِكَ لَآيَاتٍ
لِّقَوْمٍ يَتَفَكَّرُونَ

And of His signs is that He created for you from
yourselves mates that you may find tranquillity in
them; and He placed between you affection and
mercy. Indeed in that are signs for a people
who give thoughts.
(Quran 30:21)

02

Falling in love is easy but sustaining a loving relationship is hard work

The Blessed Prophet, said: "There is nothing better for two who love each other than marriage." *(Hadith Ibn Majah`)*

The advice of the Prophet was that if someone has fallen in love, they should be helped to get married. In Muslim cultures today, many people resort to all sorts of plans and schemes to prevent people getting married. For many, 'love marriage' is a dirty phrase. It does not have to be like that.

Ideally speaking, you should be objective and not blinded by your emotions when you are making such an important decision in life. The word 'love' conjures in our minds some of the following images and feelings:
- Stars in your eyes
- Butterflies in your stomach

- You can't stop thinking about her/him
- Intense feelings of happiness
- Longing to hear the voice, receive a text message or email
- Nothing seems more important than his/her company
- You have great chemistry between you and you 'click'
- You start to plan the future with him/her

Love is a verb and needs hard work. According to Kahlil Gibran; *"Work is love made visible. And if you cannot work with love but only with distaste, it is better that you should leave your work and sit at the gate of the temple and take alms of those who work with joy."* Be proud of the hard work you put in sustaining a loving relationship. It changes form with age and requires constant renewal. It goes up and down and needs reaffirming. The above list illustrates the early part of courtship but these feelings fade with time.

Islam defines love through small acts of generosity:
- Compassion and mercy
- Focusing on the good traits of your spouse
- Overlooking those traits you dislike
- Accepting and respect them for who they are
- Doing things together regularly

Love can blind you to the real character of a person. A good friend once told me 'Love is blind but the neighbours ain't!'

Once the honeymoon period is over, you may wake up realising you have made a terrible mistake! In order to avoid this try the following steps:
- Avoid making a shopping list of what you want, but make a list of what you can offer. Dreaming is good, but being realistic is essential.
- Ask for references from people who know the person well - positive and negative.

- Be absolutely honest about yourself when you discuss issues with your prospective spouse.
- Avoid pretending or making up stories about you or your family.

Allah promises His grace when two people get married and work to deepen their relationship. Islam proposes that we manifest God-consciousness in our human relationships through practical and day-to-day acts of generosity. Part of being God-conscious is to be mindful of the way we treat our spouse. When the focus of instant pleasure is away from the couple's mind, peace and love can be achieved easily. Love is a slow-release dose of pleasures in life.

Islam places a great deal of importance on practical works that cement a long-lasting relationship. The verse of the Qur'an thus talks about how Allah places love (Mawadda), compassion and mercy (Rahma) in our hearts when we work hard to find tranquillity and comfort (Sakina) in each other.

For love to flourish, it needs the couple to:
- Respect and accept each other
- Spend quality time together
- Trust each other enough to share their thoughts, show vulnerability and emotions
- Have honesty and integrity at the core of the relationship.

"The chemist who can extract from his heart's elements compassion, respect, longing, patience, regret, surprise, and forgiveness, and compound them into one, can create that atom which is called love." - Kahlil Gibran

Tips and tabs

Think about the following statement:

> *"Where there is faith, there is love.*
> *Where there is love, there is peace.*
> *Where there is peace there is God;*
> *Where there is God, there is no need."*
> - Leo Tolstoy

Key questions for you to reflect:

- Is your love blind, extreme or moderate?
- Can you love too much?
- Can you manage your love to a moderate level?
- Can your love for someone go up and down?

The Prophet loved his wives deeply, he loved his companions deeply, he loved people in his society, especially the poor and the orphans but above all he loved Allah the most. The balance between various forms of love is the key.

The blessed Prophet said: "Love the one whom you love to a certain degree (moderately), perhaps one day he/she will be someone for whom you have hatred, and hate the one for whom you have hatred to a certain degree (moderately), perhaps one day he/she will be one whom you love" *(Hadith Tirmidhi)*

The question is what should be the level of love for our spouse? Can we get it wrong - either we love someone too much or love someone too little? These are some of the key questions that we should reflect on when understanding love.

Love can be conditional or unconditional. Have you ever thought of the difference between the two? Do you know how to transform conditional love to unconditional love?

Please turn to the next page and follow a simple exercise to find out.

Exercise 1: List five examples of what in your view is conditional or unconditional love.

Conditional love	Unconditional love
I like how you make me feel	I care about how you feel

Reflect on how you can turn conditional love into unconditional love in practice.

Lover's checklist

Am I using my head or heart? Tick or cross in the boxes:

	Yes	No
I cannot see anything wrong with him/her		
I cannot stop thinking about him/her		
I cannot live without him/her		
Why is everyone against us?		
We love each other, that's all we need		
Who cares about what parents think, let's just get married or run away		
Nobody will break us apart, we were born for each other		
We are so great, we never fight		

If you have:
- More than 5 yes: You are certainly using your heart
- 3-5 yes: You are able to distinguish between heart and head
- Less than 3 yes: You are certainly using your head

> *Love is compassion, respect and small acts of generosity. Love is the bond that sustains the relationship not a spark that creates it*

إِنَّ الْمُسْلِمِينَ وَالْمُسْلِمَاتِ وَالْمُؤْمِنِينَ
وَالْمُؤْمِنَاتِ وَالْقَانِتِينَ وَالْقَانِتَاتِ وَالصَّادِقِينَ
وَالصَّادِقَاتِ وَالصَّابِرِينَ وَالصَّابِرَاتِ
وَالْخَاشِعِينَ وَالْخَاشِعَاتِ وَالْمُتَصَدِّقِينَ
وَالْمُتَصَدِّقَاتِ وَالصَّائِمِينَ وَالصَّائِمَاتِ
وَالْحَافِظِينَ فُرُوجَهُمْ وَالْحَافِظَاتِ وَالذَّاكِرِينَ
اللَّهَ كَثِيرًا وَالذَّاكِرَاتِ أَعَدَّ اللَّهُ لَهُم مَّغْفِرَةً
وَأَجْرًا عَظِيمًا

VERILY, for all men and women who have
surrendered themselves unto God, and all believing
men and believing women, and all truly devout
men and truly devout women, and all men and
women who are true to their word, and all men and
women who are patient in adversity, and all men
and women who humble themselves [before God],
and all men and women who give in charity, and all
self-denying men and self-denying women, and all
men and women who are mindful of their chastity,
[and all men and women] who remember God
unceasingly: for [all of] them has God readied
forgiveness of sins and a mighty reward.
(Quran 33:35)

03

Men and women are different

"The male is not [or "could not be"] like the female…" *(Qur'an 3:36)*

Can you imagine if we were all the same? If the world only had men or only women? Life would have come to an end and even if life continued I could only imagine it being extremely boring.

Our differences keep us alive and interesting. Our differences attract us to each other. Our differences make the world so colourful.

The male/female differences encompass not just the physiology but our spiritual being, too. We are different in our:

- Emotions and feelings
- Ways of thinking
- Logic
- Communication
- Expressions
- Perceptions

These differences do not make us better than each other. We are all equal in the eyes of Allah. In Islam, men and women are equally encouraged to seek spiritual development and fulfilment.

Knowing our differences is the key to successfully navigating and negotiating our way around in a marriage.

If you ask a man or a woman for directions, the answer is most likely to be different even though both sets of directions may eventually lead you to your desired destination. Whose directions are better? This is a wrong question. Both of them are good and valid. Knowing and accepting that there are many ways to reach the same place is the first step to a successful marriage.

What makes you happy may not make your spouse happy. There is no logical reason why it should. If you only guess what makes your spouse happy, it is most likely that you will get it wrong. Ask your spouse what makes him/her happy. Accepting this difference is essential to happiness.

Once during an argument my wife said, "Don't ask me to be logical, I am upset and I am angry! I cannot be logical right now". I was rather taken aback by her outburst but when we were calm and analysed what happened, we both realised one thing - we are different. While I was in 'problem solving' mode she was in her 'feelings' mode.

We must understand that we all have different ways of solving problems, addressing issues and responding to events. This is not about the right way or the wrong way; this is about respecting our unique ways.

For a marriage to be successful, a man does not have to give up his masculinity and dress or behave like a woman to be accepted. A woman does not need to behave like a man to be given her fair worth.

Knowing that we are different and learning how to relate to each other is essential to developing a meaningful marital relationship.

Allah in His infinite wisdom has made us different so that we would respect and accept each other. To be prejudiced based on gender is to be prejudiced against Allah. Islam proposes a holistic gender balance creating a more harmonious co-existence between men and women.

There is no need to wage a 'gender jihad' in a marriage; there is a need for understanding our uniqueness and complementary roles. The blessed Prophet once said:

"Verily, women are the twin halves of men."

(Hadith Abu Dawood)

Tips and tabs

The table below contains a list of differing tendencies between men and women based on personal observations.

Men tend to:	Women tend to:
Prioritise logic over emotions	Prioritise emotions over logic
Need a reason for talking	Need no reason to talk
Use 95% of their attention	Use 100% of their attention
Do one thing at a time	Can multitask and multi-think
Do not like questions	Love questions
Like to forget	Like to remember
Long for appreciation	Long for understanding
Want solutions	Do not need immediate solutions
Use one part of their brain at any given time	Use their whole brain to experience
Value efficiency above all	Value happiness above all
Be getters	Be givers
Want to be right	Keep scores
Like big ideas	Like small details
Want a peaceful life without much hassle	Make a big deal out of small things

Of course there are exceptions to every generalisation. This list is not exhaustive and I am sure you will find your own items from your own experience. I have only included it here as a pointer to understand our differences. It only shows that there are substantial differences between men and women at every level.

Knowing and being comfortable with our differences is the key to a successful a marriage.

وَمِنْ آيَاتِهِ أَنْ خَلَقَ لَكُم مِّنْ أَنفُسِكُمْ
أَزْوَاجًا لِّتَسْكُنُوا إِلَيْهَا وَجَعَلَ بَيْنَكُم
مَّوَدَّةً وَرَحْمَةً إِنَّ فِي ذَٰلِكَ لَآيَاتٍ
لِّقَوْمٍ يَتَفَكَّرُونَ

And in everything have We created opposites, so
that you might bear in mind
[that God alone is One].
(Quran 51:49)

04

Marriage is half of your religion but he/she is not the other half

"They are as a garment for you and you are as a garment for them" *(Quran 2:187)*

Marriage is a partnership between two people and this partnership is likened by Allah to a garment. I find this illustration most beautiful and befitting because garments usually:
- Protect us from the weather
- Hide our imperfections and shame
- Protect our privacy
- Beautify us

The marital relationship is like a garment that fits comfortably and the fit is unique to our individual shapes and sizes. Each and every garment I wear has a unique feature. While it beautifies me, it never loses its individual identity. In marriage, the partnership is about team work but individual identity should not be lost in the process.

The role of a garment is to complement our looks. The husband and wife's roles in a marriage is similarly complementary. Complementary attributes include:

- **Support** – Providing support where support is needed, as opposed to taking over. You need to lend a hand when asked.

- **Understanding** – Supportive of each other's ambitions and aims in life. You need to understand each other's dreams.

- **Not 'point scoring'** – All discussions do not have to end in arguments or be about who won the debate or who scored the last or final point.

- Being **mutual consciousness of each other's wellbeing** – It's not only your desires and welfare that require attention, your spouse also has needs. Mutual wellbeing, physical and spiritual, are at the core of your relationship.

- **Bringing out the best in each other** – Nurturing and encouraging wholesome growth and progression in marital life is also a key ingredient for a lasting relationship. A stale and stagnant relationship is soul-destroying.

- **Complementarily in skills and attributes** – In any partnership, identifying the strengths and weaknesses is the beginning of a flourishing adventure. Marriage is no different. You should meet the skills gap of each other and where development is needed you seek it.

Men and women are equal in the eyes of Allah. Our spiritual status is equal and we will gain the fair due of our devotion. "And thus does their Sustainer answer their prayer: "I shall not lose sight of the labour of any of you who work hard in My way, be it man or woman: each of you is an issue of the other". *(Quran 3:195)*

Our efforts are rewarded regardless of male female status and we are all members of one and the same human race, and therefore equal to one another.

Men are not superior to women. Leadership of the family should not be imposed like a dictator; it should be earned and entrusted. Men who demand loyalty and subjugate women are the least qualified to lead their family. Marital partnership is consensual, not authoritarian.

There are two specific roles to be performed in a marriage: bread-wining and homemaking. The question of who delivers them is obvious in the Islamic tradition. However, nowadays this is often questioned, challenged or even belittled. Once you have delivered on those divinely ordained roles you can negotiate with your spouse to take up any other roles.

Through marriage we build comfortable environments in which to enjoy the relationship. When faced with challenges we are encouraged to reconcile and not break up the partnership readily.

"The believers are but brothers. So make peace between your brothers, and remain conscious of God that you may receive His mercy." *(Qur'an 49:10)*

In a marriage we seek to build that peaceful, fulfilling and happy environment. Key to making peace at home is negotiating and compromising as often as possible. Enjoy the partnership, invest in it, you shall reap the benefits.

Tips and tabs

Exercise 1:
Understanding my spouse or my potential spouse

Take a note book and write down specific things about your spouse. Please be very specific in your observation and focus on your partnership.

- What do you most like about your partner i.e. skills, attributes and specific talents?
- What do you most dislike about your partner?
- How does your partner react to various situations?
- How many times does your spouse get upset?
- Do you notice any changes in his/her body-language or facial expressions?
- How often does your partner complain?
- How often does your partner compliment you?
- How well do you work together?

Once you have written down the observation please focus on yourself. Ask yourself the following questions and note your observations:

- What does your partner most like about you i.e. skills, attributes and specific talents?
- What does your partner most dislike about you?
- How do you react to various situations?
- How often do you get upset?
- Do you notice any changes in your body-language or facial expressions? Does your partner notice them?
- How often do you complain?
- How often do you compliment your partner?

As you study your notes, you should be able to develop common features of this partnership. List below 3 common traits of your partnership (marital or potential):

1.

2.

3.

Please place a tick in the appropriate box below:

Checklist - Are you a control-freak or a team-player?

Control-freaks:

	True	False
I am bossy and domineering. I find it difficult to delegate – "If you want it done right, you have to do it yourself!"		
I verbally and mentally bully or manipulate people into submission using fear, guilt or intimidation - even exaggerating issues to have better control of the situation		
I am a perfectionist – "it's my way or the highway." I have to have the last say in everything and refuse to listen to anyone else's point of view		
I sulk and pout and generally make everyone's life miserable until I have my way or people simply give in to me		
I can make attention and affection conditional on compliance		
I can use passive aggression - involving intentional procrastination and deliberate stubbornness		
I elittle others - with the intention to destroy confidence and make them weak and dependent		
I tend to control the finances and decide on what or what not to buy		

On a seperate piece of paper list one specific task that you can do for each of the control-freak traits that you have indentified in yourself so that you can become a team player.

Team-players:

✓ Are willing to negotiate, demonstrate flexibility and adaptability
✓ Look for the common good of all parties and not just themselves
✓ Are altruistic - selfless and non-egotistical; at the core of their motivation is to genuinely serve others
✓ Are dependable with clear intentions, motivation and have sound judgement
✓ Are responsible in delivering the allotted or assigned task. They never let the team down!

The ideal position is to be a team-player and not a control-freak. To change is possible – but you have to be willing to make the change.

> You are both part of the same team in your marriage, play to your strengths.

يَا أَيُّهَا الَّذِينَ أَمَنُوا لِمَ تَقُولُونَ مَا لَا تَفْعَلُونَ

O YOU who have attained to faith!
Why do you say one thing and do another?
(Quran 61:2)

05

It is clever to know what you are looking for but it is foolish not to know what you are offering

"None of you have perfected your faith until he wishes for his brother what he wishes for yourself." *(Hadith Bukhari)*

Wishing for others what you would like for yourself is probably the hardest thing to do in life. In marriage this principle forms the cornerstone for a sharing and caring culture. It means being willing to give more than you receive. If you cannot do that, at least give as much as you take.

When you are looking for someone to marry ask yourself this most important question: Do I know what I am offering and what I am looking for?

Are you looking for a person who:

- Would clean, cook and iron for you
- Would pick up the pieces behind you
- Would put up with your aimless life
- A person who can give you love and support regardless of what you do or say
- A person who will always be there, no matter what

Parents might recognise such features in their children! If this is what you are looking for, you may be confusing your expectations. Please note a wife is not a replacement for a mother and a husband is not a replacement for a father!

Many of us have expectations that are based on Hollywood or Bollywood films, wild fantasies or unfulfilled dreams and desires.

Unfortunately, unrealistic expectations are among the greatest causes of strife and pain in marriages. Expectations are the cousins of control-freakery.

Think about the following issues:

- **Perfection:** I am looking for a perfect woman or man, Mr or Miss Right, the most handsome man or the most beautiful woman. I am looking for my "soul mate"!

In our hearts we know that the contemporary populist images we all hold in our hearts are, in reality, fantasies! No two people are alike, we are all imperfect, we are all human beings. We have to accept realities around us and about us!

- **Similarity:** "He may not go shopping with me", "She doesn't think like me", "We are so similar I even know what he is thinking" and "Unless we are similar we may face problems".

Have you ever heard these sentiments expressed? If you were so similar you would probably get bored with each other very quickly. Diversity is the key for a healthy relationship. Only Allah knows what is in our minds; we can never read minds!

- **Romance:** "Eventually, he won't bring me flowers so often" or "She may not make as much effort for me as she did before".

This is absolutely true! This is what happens in life, you cannot change that. Turn romance into a living reality through continuous, small acts of generosity, kind words, simple touches and reassurances. Romance is not rocket science!

- **Change:** "She will change"; "I will change him".

Never demand change from others. Accepting the person for who they are, in their entirety, is the only way fulfilling relationships are developed and nurtured. If someone wishes to change, it is entirely a personal choice; imposed changes only leave trails of anger and resentment. It is short-lived and should never be encouraged.

- **Fulfilment:** "You complete me", "Without you my life is worthless" or "I would die without you".

Such ideas are not a good philosophy for a healthy and fulfilling relationship. No one ever dies because their spouse has left them or has died. Life goes on beyond our marriages. One of my teachers use to say to me "get a grip on yourself and start to live and enjoy life through your marriage."

One golden tip I was given when I was looking to get married is - know what you are offering before you ask what is on offer.

Tips and tabs

*Tell the truth about yourself so you can find people
who will love you.
Tell the truth and it will encourage people to tell the
truth about themselves.*

Exercise 1: List 10 truths about yourself you are only
willing to share with your spouse/potential spouse.
Write down 10 truths about yourself in the table
below or on a separate piece of paper:

	Truth about me
1	
2	
3	
4	
5	
6	
7	
8	
9	
10	

Please take a moment and reflect on your feelings about what you have written and your feeling on sharing it.

Telling other people about ourselves is daunting at the easiest of times; it may be even more unsettling to open the stories of our life to a spouse or potential spouse. So if you feel uncomfortable or disturbed by the exercise please talk to a friend or someone you trust.

Exercise 2: We all bring something to the world that is unique. A flourishing relationship can bring the best out of us. Write up an advert about yourself. Focus on what it is that you bring to your partner/potential partner that makes you unique? What are you willing to bring to the marriage table? Maximum 300 words...

I am ...

Share your advert with a close friend, take his/her feedback. If you are not honest in the advert, the likely outcome would also be dishonest. You certainly do not want to start a marriage on a false note!

Exercise 3: Please place a tick under the number that corresponds to the order of importance to you (1 is least important and 5 is most):

	Expectations	1	2	3	4	5
1	My spouse should make a good impression on other people					
2	My spouse should be artistic					
3	My spouse should have academic qualifications					
4	My spouse should have brown eyes					
5	My spouse must wear hijab/beard					
6	My spouse should be attractive according to other people					
7	I would like my spouse to be a good educator					
8	Height is important to me					
9	I would like a sociable spouse					
10	I can see my future spouse as a father/mother of our children					
11	Body shape is important					
12	My spouse should be respected					
13	I would like my spouse to be honest					
14	I prefer a spouse who is good with money					
15	My spouse should have practical skills					
16	My spouse should have a profession					
17	My spouse must be tall					

If you have scored high for the questions -

1, 7, 9, 10, 12 and 13 you are **personality driven**
4, 5, 6, 8, 11 and 17 you are **look driven**
2, 3, 14, 15 and 16 you are **achievement driven**

> Honesty is the best policy, without it you create more trouble for yourself and your spouse.

اللَّهُ الَّذِي جَعَلَ لَكُمُ الْأَرْضَ قَرَارًا
وَالسَّمَاء بِنَاء وَصَوَّرَكُمْ فَأَحْسَنَ صُوَرَكُمْ
وَرَزَقَكُم مِّنَ الطَّيِّبَاتِ ذَلِكُمُ اللَّهُ رَبُّكُمْ
فَتَبَارَكَ اللَّهُ رَبُّ الْعَالَمِينَ

It is God who has made the earth a resting- place
for you and the sky a canopy, and has formed you -
and formed you so well and provided for you
sustenance out of the good things of life. Such is
God, your Sustainer: hallowed, then, is God, the
Sustainer of all the worlds!
(Quran 40:64)

06

Looks are important but not as important as personality

"A woman may be married for four reasons: for her property, her status, her beauty, and her piety; so try to get one who is pious, may you be blessed." *(Hadith Bukhari)*

In life status and wealth fluctuate! I know many people who were wealthy one day and penniless the next. We all know people who were powerful one day and insignificant the next. Such short-term criteria cannot be good enough reasons for marriage. In fact, I also happen to know many people who have gained status and wealth as a result of the bliss, happiness and contentment they experienced in a fulfilling marriage, with a supportive spouse.

Islam transcends tribal identity, ethnic boundaries, linage, nationality, colour, race and language. Those who profess this faith belong to a universal community. Marriage between and across cultural divides should be greatly encouraged as the Blessed Prophet advised us to marry people from afar. Of course, the gene pool in cross- cultural marriages is far richer and reduces the risk of hereditary illnesses in the offspring. I am a British Bangladeshi, my wife is Hungarian; our cultural differences have been our strength and source of great joy and honour. Racism when choosing a spouse for marriage should never be tolerated.

Now let us examine the concept of looks and beauty, one of the most contentious issues that make or break many marriage prospects. Are looks a very important criteria for you? Ask yourself – "What influences my perception of what is beautiful? How do I define good looks?"

- Looks are skin-deep
- Looks become boring after a while
- Looks naturally fade away
- Looks can be deceptive

"Beauty is in the eye of the beholder" – that everyone should accept us for who we are and not how we look, would be a fair interpretation of this phrase.

Allah expresses His beauty through his attributes, more commonly known as the 99 beautiful names. The true and lasting beauty of a person lies in their heart and conduct, and not the face or the body.

"Verily Allah does not look to your bodies nor to your faces but He looks to your hearts," and in another narration, "Verily Allah does not look to your faces and your wealth but He looks to your heart and to your deeds." *(Hadith Muslim)*

In the search for a suitable spouse, your focus should

always be beyond the face and body. You should look at the personality and character of the person. The key questions that you should reflect on are:

- How does this person deal with people, family, friends and general public?
- Does this person know how to deal with anger?
- Is this person in debt and how do they manage their financial affairs?
- Is this person honest and upright?
- What do others think about this person?

Many people become so blinded by the dazzling beauty and the good looks of the person they are considering, that they forget to explore the character in detail – something that is often regretted later. They forget to consider issues of personality and compatibility.

The best thing you can do is to ask trusted family members or friends who know the person in question. Ask more than one person for positive and negative feedback. Of course you will do this with the intention of marrying and not to spread gossip about them. When asking, tell them that the information will of course, as is the Islamic manner, be personal to you and not divulged even to the intended.

The inner beauty of a human being is most pleasant: it is calming to the eyes and contenting to the heart. Why get stung by outer appearances?

You may fall in love with the beauty of the person but you have to live with the character

Tips and tabs

God, grant me the serenity
To accept the things I cannot change;
Courage to change the things I can;
And wisdom to know the difference.
(Reinhold Niebuhr)

Compatibility checklist

Indicators	yes	no
Our profession, work or career is compatible		
We have similar or complementary views and attitudes to managing finances		
We actively support humanitarian causes		
We have similar family backgrounds		
We can cope with family differences		
We are compatible in our approach to religion		
We both focus on personal growth		
We have similar understanding of what constitutes a healthy lifestyle		
Our approach to social life is compatible		
We share common interests in recreation and leisure		
Our political ideologies are similar		

If you have:
0 - 4 ticks for Yes: You will be struggling
5-8: You need to carefully negotiate
9-11: You seem to be compatible

All the above are compatibility indicators that people who are interested in getting married need to seriously consider. Similarity in everything is not an indicator of compatibility. Differences could be equally compatible. However, in each case, whether similar or different, the people concerned should be prepared to negotiate and learn how to manage issues. One size fits all should never be the approach.

الآنَ بَاشِرُوهُنَّ وَابْتَغُواْ مَا كَتَبَ اللّهُ لَكُمْ

Now, then, you may lie with them skin to skin,
and avail yourselves of that which
God has ordained for you
(Quran 2:187)

07

Marriage is not all about sex, but sex is an essential part of a healthy relationship

"In the sexual act of each of you there is a sadaqa."
The Companions replied: "O Messenger of Allah!
When one of us fulfils his sexual desire, will he be
given a reward for that?" And he said, "Do you not
think that were he to act upon it unlawfully,
he would be sinning? Likewise, if he acts upon it
lawfully he will be rewarded."
(Hadith Muslim)

We all know that sex outside marriage is strictly forbidden in Islam. The verse of the Quran is explicit and makes forbidden for anyone to even go near sex outside marriage. "Do not even go near Zina" (Quran 17:32), thus intensifying the prohibition. It is to be noted that the term zina signifies all sexual intercourse between a man and a woman who are not husband and wife, irrespective of whether either of them is married to another partner or not; hence, it denotes both "adultery" and "fornication" in the English senses of these terms.

There is also a very clear statement of the blessed Prophet reminding us of the grave consequences: "There is no greater sin after the sin of associating partners with Allah, than a man placing his semen in a womb [private part of a woman] that is unlawful for him to place".*(Hadith Ahmad)*

Yet the over-sexualised society around us makes it extremely difficult for anyone to remain sexually inactive and wait until marriage. I am not condoning such illicit behaviour nor am I turning a blind eye to it. I would like to focus on the issues of sex and intimacy in this chapter.

Amongst Allah's greatest gifts to human beings is sex. He has made humans fundamentally sexual beings. Through sex we express our innermost love and intimacy with someone we are in a committed relationship with. One night stands, casual sex, no strings attached (NSA) sex, pay as you go sex or short term temporary marriage contracts are some examples of how sex has been reduced to a material function rather an expression of deeply held feelings in a loving and committed relationship.

Islam does not consider sex as taboo or dirty. You are allowed to talk about it, but using decent language, not vulgarity. Sex is considered a form of worship that is rewarded if enjoyed with the right person.

"A person who would have sex with his spouse would be rewarded for it. The Companions asked: 'Oh Messenger of Allah! A person would be rewarded while satisfying his sexual need?' Allah's Blessed Messenger replied: 'Yes. Isn't it that he would be punished if he had sex illegally? The same applies if a believer had sex lawfully with his spouse. As such, he would be rewarded" *(Hadith Ahmad)*

The Islamic marriage contract gives license to the husband and wife to mutual sexual gratification and pleasure. It legitimises their relationship and places both legal and moral responsibility on the couple in the case of children.

Before I write about sex in more details I would like to mention one even more important issue that I believe many Muslim families, due to cultural reasons, seriously lack – knowledge of intimacy and how to express it. Most of us do not know how to express it and do not appreciate it when it is being expressed.

Intimacy has various levels; at the most basic level would be gentle and light expressions through a gentle kiss, touch, holding hands, hugs and kind and tender words. These are expressions that can be expressed at home in front of children or in public - in moderation, or course! The higher level of intimacy is private between the spouses expressed more frequently would strengthen the relationship.

Intimacy can be expressed through sex, though not exclusively. Appreciate your spouse and reassure each other of your love and commitment by saying simple yet very powerful words generously – "I love you", "You look beautiful", "I like what you are doing to me" and "That feels wonderful" or anything else that you like.

Intimacy makes sex more pleasurable. Before you jump into sex, prepare for it, take your time and enjoy it. The Prophet advised us; "One of you should not fulfil your sexual need from your wife like an animal, rather there should be between you foreplay of kissing and words."

There are some key issues you need to consider when it comes to sex:

Sex is for mutual pleasure – mutual satisfaction is imperative for a meaningful and fulfilling relationship. Don't just satisfy your needs and fall asleep. Some men pay little attention to the sexual pleasure of their wife; as soon as they have reached their climax they usually turn over and fall asleep. This is a most unfair and unkind gesture towards someone you deeply love. Ask your wife what you could do to satisfy her, to bring her to an orgasm. What would she like? Being open and honest with each other is essential to a fulfilling sex life and lasting contentment.

Sex is a divine gift:

Allah is the Creator; he has delegated the responsibility of procreation on our shoulders. He has gifted sex as a means to procreation. There is a deep sense of spiritual journey in sex and that awareness will help strengthen the couple's relationship and enable them to enjoy the divine gift adequately.

Good practice tips:

We find in the Quran using metaphor of the land when describing the conjugal relationship between husband and wife "Your wives are your tilth; go, then, unto your tilth as you may desire, but first provide something for your souls" *(Quran 2:223)*

This verse brings to our mind the image of a farmer attending his field. The best farmer is he who takes care of his farm, sows seeds to reap great harvest. He would not sow it without preparing the land or outside the right season. He would tend to it in a manner which will not cause injury or exhaust the soil. He will be wise and considerate and certainly will not intend to damage the land.

A spiritual relationship between man and woman is suggested as the indispensable basis of sexual relations. The relationship is tender, caring and mutual.

- **Prepare for it:** brush your teeth, for bad breath could be most off putting at the height of pleasure; wash your private parts if you suspect the area to be not as clean as you would like; wear nice fragrances that are pleasurable and attractive mutually; dress up - wear nice and sexy clothes. Seduce your spouse and enjoy every minute of it.

- **Kiss and caress for a reasonable amount of time:** A man's arousal is centred on his erection which can be sustained through touch; a woman's state of arousal is rooted in the kisses and caresses; the outcome is a woman's vagina secretes natural lubricant allowing easier penetration. It can be very painful for a woman if she is not ready and a man penetrates her. At the state of arousal the whole body is longing for touch.

  Exchange passionate kisses or French kiss as more commonly known today - the blessed Prophet used to practice this with his wives. The sexually aroused spouse is like a guitar, you can play the most beautiful notes if you pull the right strings. It is Allah's immense grace, so appreciate it and enjoy it.

- **Be sensitive to the response of your spouse:** If your spouse is enjoying what you are doing you will hear moans or sounds of joy. If you hear or see discomfort, stop and ask, change what you are doing. Do not be fixated on your pleasure only.

- **Sex between couples has no rules:** As long as you do not harm each other and sexual activities are consensual, a couple can approach and play with each other in any way they choose. There are traditions of the blessed Prophet that make anal sex unlawful, but, apart from that, the sky is the limit.

- **Climax together:** Sexual pleasure peaks for a couple at the moment of orgasm. Not all spouses can achieve orgasm at the same time, all the time. If you achieve orgasm first and if you could not delay until your spouse was on the same level, help to satisfy your spouse later. There are many ways to reach the same point, and since there is no limit to what you can do. Experiment together.

- **Spend post-coital moments together:** Sexual pleasure does not end with orgasm or ejaculation. Bask in the glory of orgasm, hold each other, rest and drift away in sweet slumber. Appreciate the most physical and metaphysical experiences blended in one earth-shattering climax you have just enjoyed. Thank your spouse for it and thank Allah for His grace. Some men develop a hatred for a woman after ejaculation and it is clinically known as post-coital hatred. This usually happens in loveless sex, one-night stands and casual sex. It is a terrible way to end one of greatest gift of God.

Remember, to think about the need of your spouse, a sexually-frustrated spouse may also be an angry, resentful and unfriendly spouse!

Tips and tabs

"With passion pray, with passion make love, with passion eat and drink and dance and play. Why act like a dead fish in this ocean of God?"
-Rumi

Checklist:

Please take a few minutes, reflect on the following issues that have been listed, place a tick if you agree or cross if you disagree under the appropriate status box:

	Yes	No
I am comfortable with my private parts? (The way they look, feel and the size)		
I have sufficient knowledge of the anatomy of the opposite sex		
I understand the nature of sex in the marital relationship		
I believe having sex with a spouse in the nude is not allowed in Islam		
I am willing to explore all aspects of sex with my spouse		
I understand that intimacy also means moderate display of affection such as hugs, strokes and gentle kisses		
I understand what is meant by foreplay		
I understand that both men and women achieve sexual orgasms		
I know erection is a definite sign of a man's arousal		
I believe oral sex is not allowed		
Islam places strict rules around how we have sex with our spouse		

If you have:

less then 3 ticks you need to read up on this topic
4-7 ticks your knowledge is average, read further
8-11 ticks you have good knowledge

If you need to brush up on your sexual confidence and knowledge buy a good book on sex and Islam. Read it with your spouse; make it part of mutual learning and fun.

> Sex is a gift from Allah; it is fun and a great way to explore depth in a relationship.

وَقُولُواْ لِلنَّاسِ حُسْناً

Speak to all people in the most kindly manner
(Quran 2:83)

08

You may know how to talk but do you know how to communicate?

> "O you who have attained to faith! Remain conscious of God, and always speak with a will to bring out [only] what is just and true. He will cause your deeds to be virtuous, and will forgive you your sins. And [know that] whoever pays heed unto God and His Apostle has already attained to a mighty triumph." *(Quran 33:70-71)*

There is a famous saying that you have two ears and one mouth, use them in that proportion. Some people love the sound of their own voice. The art of good communication is to say what you mean and be heard in the way you want to be heard. The blessed Prophet reminds us that "Even a pleasant word is charity".

Good communication is not:
- When you shout the loudest
- When you argue the most
- When you ignore the opinion of others
- When you always get your way

There are five principles that govern good communication:

i) **Listen carefully:** When someone is talking to you, it is important that your body language demonstrates you are actually listening. You should pay attention to what is being said and show empathy.

ii) **Say what you mean and mean what you say:** If you do not mean it, do not say it, would be the best advice. Words make and break relationships, so say things that will bring the best out of your spouse. Some go too far, using words intended to hurt and cause maximum damage. This is not the best way to communicate, especially not with the person you love!

iii) **Do not judge another's intention:** You cannot read minds, therefore do not interpret what is being said using your own biased thoughts. Ask your spouse what the intention was behind what was said. It is reported that the blessed Prophet reminds us that we should give the benefit of the doubt even seventy times.

iv) **Give feedback:** Clarify if you feel you have been misunderstood or not heard right , or if you have not heard something correctly. One way to ensure this happens effectively is to simply say, "Did I hear you right, did you say..." or "Did you mean" or "Let me clarify" or "I may have said it wrong, let me say that again". These small phrases avoid huge upheavals and hurt feelings. Express how you feel honestly and respectfully. If your spouse does not know how you feel, how will they address the issue?

v) **Agree on a resolution:** At the end of any conversation, especially a contentious one, do not leave it hanging. Agree on a step forward. It could be as simple as saying "Let's carry on with this conversation later" or "The way forward on the issue we have discussed is…." Take responsibility, agree on who is going to do what. A conversation that does not end with an agreed resolution usually festers and later turns into a row.

Islam places further emphasis on one more principle:

vi) **Practice what you preach:** "O YOU who have attained to faith! Why do you say one thing and do another? Most loathsome is it in the sight of God that you say what you do not do!" *(Qur'an 61:2-3)*

People who preach what they do not practice lose respect and credibility. Our loved ones pick up on these obvious contradictions and may harbour negative or ill feelings towards us. This is not the best way to develop respect and get closer to your spouse.

We should not communicate with malice in our heart. We should not harbour suspicions and doubts about our spouse. We should think well of others and speak politely or stay quiet, advised the blessed Prophet.

A saying of the blessed Prophet highlights the importance of meaningful communication:

"I guarantee a house in the surroundings [outskirts] of Paradise for a person who avoids quarrelling even if s/he were in the right; a house in the middle of Paradise for a person who avoids lying even if s/he were joking; and a house in the upper part of Paradise for a person who made her/his character good." *[Hadith Abu Dawud]*

Tips and tabs

Exercise 1: Listening practice

This task requires two people and a timer. You need to find a practice partner; ask a friend, a family member or if you are married, your spouse to help you with this exercise:

Ask your practice partner to talk about you for five minutes (strictly timed); they should only speak about your negative traits and what they most dislike about you.

You are not allowed to respond, you must listen carefully and attentively.

Exercise 2: Responding practice

This task again requires two people and a timer. Ask the same practice partner to now listen to your replies for two minutes:

It is your turn now to reply to things that have been said about you. You are only allowed two minutes and strictly time it. You can defend yourself, justify yourself, you can explain yourself or simply ignore what is being said. But it is your turn to respond for two minutes.

Please note:

- When talking or listening, eye contact is essential
- When you are listening, give feedback in the form of nods and shakes
- When you are talking, engage with the person, keep them interested in what you are saying
- When you are responding, be mindful of your body language. It is not just what you say, it is how you say it that conveys your real feelings.
- Respecting the view of those you disagree with is very important; remember, disrespect is clearly visible. Other can see it and feel it.

Communication checklist:

Please tick if you agree and cross if you disagree

	Yes	No
I speak slowly		
I am able to explain myself well		
I keep regular eye-contact with the person I am speaking to		
I don't repeat myself		
I don't raise my voice to get heard		
I mean what I say and I say what I mean		
I listen attentively		
I allow others to finish their point		
I show empathy to other views even if I disagree		
I give feedback through my body-language		
I like the sound of my own voice		
I do not dismiss other's opinions		
I like to be noticed		
I keep to the topic		
I do not mock others		
I do not use sarcasm to ridicule others		
I do not personalise a disagreement		
I am direct with my speech, even if it hurts		
I am passionate about my view		

If you have:
0-7 ticks: Your communication skills are poor
8-13 ticks: Your communication skills are average
14-19 ticks: Your communication skills are very
good

If you feel your communication skills need brushing up, there are many courses that are available. Enrol in one and you will see the benefits immediately.

We are endowed with language and the ability to express ourselves, enhancing it will only enhance our relationship, especially with our spouse.

> Successful communication is when you get your message across succinctly and allow your listeners to hear what you want them to hear.

الْمَالُ وَالْبَنُونَ زِينَةُ الْحَيَاةِ الدُّنْيَا وَالْبَاقِيَاتُ الصَّالِحَاتُ خَيْرٌ عِندَ رَبِّكَ ثَوَابًا وَخَيْرٌ أَمَلًا

Wealth and children are an adornment of this,
world's life: but good deeds, the fruit whereof
endures forever, are of far greater merit in thy
Sustainer's sight, and a far better source of hope.
(Quran: 18:46)

09

Marriage changes life and children change marriage

"You all are shepherds. You are responsible for those whom you guard. A state chieftain is responsible for those who are under his rule. An individual is obliged to protect and take care of his children and is responsible for them. A woman is responsible for her husband's home..." *(Hadith Muslim)*

I was present at the birth of our first child - Noora. Witnessing a prolonged period of agonising delivery pain, I was left humbled and speechless. My view of women permanently changed.

I was holding on to our bundle of joy when my mother walked in. As soon as I saw her, I burst into tears saying "Mum, if I have given you similar pain during my birth, I am really sorry." She smiled and said; "Your wife was in labour for 12 hours; I was in it for three days. Your wife was surrounded by midwives and doctors; I was stuck in a mud hut in the middle of a remote village. Your wife is in a hospital but I was delivering you in the middle of a war zone" (1971 war between Bangladesh and

Pakistan). I wept even more! There was nothing I could do or say. I understood the value of parents that day.

The arrival of children in a marriage changes everything. The focus shifts from the couple to the newborn. The wife becomes completely subsumed by the mothering role and the father usually trots along in a supportive role. The bulk of the work falls on the shoulder of the mother and this is naturally so. The child is extremely distraught if the link with the mother is disturbed. Islam demands that the link should never be severed or compromised. Mothers are natural homemakers.

In many cases the fathers may feel left out of the whole process, so it is important for the couple to discuss and agree on how they are going to share some of the parenting roles from the day the child is born. Failure to negotiate from the beginning may cause resentment, jealousy, and in some cases the breakdown of the relationship.

Children require a better state of preparedness on the part of the parents.

Please remember:

- To mentally prepare for a profound change
- Your life will not be the same again
- To Invest in acquiring basic knowledge about parenting through books and courses

Children bring out of parents a level of honesty and connectivity that is otherwise impossible. Children, through their innocence, teach adults about their shortcomings and failures; they mirror our characteristics and behaviour and they inspire us to become better role-models for them.

'Ali is reported to have said, "Give your children aged between 0-7 information; between 7-14 teach them discipline, boundaries and reason; and from 14 onwards be their best friend." A good start to life is all that is required of parents, yet many fail.

One day a man came to Umar ibn al-Khattab to complain about a disobedient son. So Umar had the boy brought to him and admonished him for his disobedience. The boy addressed Umar saying "O leader of the believers: Are there no rights for a boy against his father?" Umar said "Yes". Then the boy said "What are these rights, O leader of the believers?" Umar said, "To choose a good mother for him, to select a good name for him, and to teach him the Quran" Then the boy said: "O leader of the believers: my father has not accomplished any of these rights. As for my mother, she was a slave of a Magian; as for my name, he has named me Jual (beetle); and he has not taught me even one letter of the Quran". Then Umar turned round to the man and said "You came to me complaining about disobedience on the part of your son, whereas you have not given him his rights. So you have wronged him before he has wronged you."

Children need a good start to life. A good name, education, clear moral boundaries and love are the key ingredients to a sound start to life. The Prophet took a child in his lap ... and the child urinated on him, so he asked for water to wash the urine away. Embarrassed, the father sprang forward. "What have you done, you silly boy!", he shouted. His arm shoved forward to grab the child away from Muhammad, his face red with anger. Fear and confusion showed on the face of the child. The blessed Prophet restrained the man, and gently hugged the child to him. "Don't worry," he told the over-zealous father. "This is not a big issue. My clothes can be washed. But be careful with how you treat the child" he continued. "What can restore his self-esteem after you have dealt with him in public like this?" *(Hadith Bukhari)*

Self-esteem and respect are two features that start developing in the character of children from a very young age. Abu Hurairah reported: The blessed Prophet kissed his grandson Al-Hasan bin `Ali in the presence of Al-Aqra` bin Habis. Thereupon he remarked: "I have ten children and I have never kissed any one of them." The Messenger of Allah (Muhammad) looked at him and said, "He who does not show mercy to others will not be shown mercy by Allah". *(Hadith Bukhari)*

Children deserve respect and must feel they are loved.

Many children in our society grow up without simple things in life such as a warm and loving hug, words of reassurance and a sense of security. Give them love and honour when they are young and they will give you the world when you are old.

Tip and tabs

Check list:

Are you familiar with these? Please place a tick if you agree or cross if you disagree

	Yes	No
I am ready to have children		
I understand the responsibility of being a parent		
I know young children equal many sleepless nights		
Parenthood has no break – once a parent, always a parent		
You cannot wish a crying baby to be quiet, if the baby is distressed, crying is all it can do		
Babies need nappy changes frequently and you do not have a say over this		
Babies need frequent feeding and you do not have a say over this		
Babies make mess		
Babies have feelings		

If you have

0-3 tick: You are not ready to have children
4-6 ticks: You are familiar with parenting
7-9 ticks: You are ready to have children

Exercise 1:

Discuss your thoughts and feelings; say to your spouse "I would like to have a child of my own"

Now discuss the following questions:

- How many kids do we envision having?
- Who would wake up throughout the night to attend the baby?
- What lifestyle changes will we need to make when we become parents?
- Can we cope by ourselves or do we need to secure help first?
- What name should we give the child?

Note down your responses, discuss common grounds and disagreements and develop a mutually satisfactory outcome to the above raised questions.

> Children learn from examples, so be the best role model for them

وَقَضَى رَبُّكَ أَلاَّ تَعْبُدُواْ إِلاَّ إِيَّاهُ وَبِالْوَالِدَيْنِ
إِحْسَانًا إِمَّا يَبْلُغَنَّ عِندَكَ الْكِبَرَ أَحَدُهُمَا أَوْ
كِلاَهُمَا فَلاَ تَقُل لَّهُمَآ أُفٍّ وَلاَ تَنْهَرْهُمَا وَقُل
لَّهُمَا قَوْلاً كَرِيمًاوَاخْفِضْ لَهُمَا جَنَاحَ الذُّلِّ
مِنَ الرَّحْمَةِ وَقُل رَّبِّ ارْحَمْهُمَا كَمَا
رَبَّيَانِي صَغِيرًا

For thy Sustainer has ordained that you shall
worship none but Him. And do good unto [thy]
parents. Should one of them, or both, attain to old
age in thy care, never say "Ugh" to them or scold
them, but [always] speak unto them with reverent
speech. And spread over them humbly the wings of
thy tenderness, and say: "O my Sustainer! Bestow
Thy grace upon them, even as they cherished and
reared me when I was a child!
(*Quran 17:23-24*)

10

Should in-laws be outlaws?

One who reciprocates benevolence is not the one
who upholds the ties of kinship. The one who
upholds the ties of kinship is the one who is kind to
his/her relatives even when they are hostile.
(Hadith Bukhari)

Your spouse is someone's son or daughter. Your
spouse has parents and thus has obligations towards
them. In Islam, the second most important
obligation after that towards Allah is to honour our
parents.

The blessed Prophet warned us against neglecting our
parents. He said: "Let that man be disgraced; and
disgraced again and let him be disgraced even more."
The people enquired: "O Prophet of God, who is that
man?" The blessed Prophet responded: "I refer to the
man who finds his parents old in age - both of them
or one of them - and yet did not earn entitlement to
Paradise by rendering good service to them."

(Hadith Muslim)

Helping your spouse fulfil his or her obligations towards parents is not only sensible but a sign of purity of heart and generosity in your nature. I am sure we would not like our spouses to be disgraced in this world and certainly not in the Hereafter. In a relationship, supporting each other is essential, and with those we love it is most sensible.

In an argument, some people do not think about what they say. In the heat of the moment, a couple can lose all sense of restraint and throw the most hurtful words at each other, often related to the in-laws. Are you familiar with the following kinds of statements?

- ✗ It is either me or your mother - you had better choose!
- ✗ I cannot stand your parents, please do not ask me to visit them!
- ✗ Your mother is a witch; she drives me up the wall!
- ✗ I am never going to live with your parents!
- ✗ He is your father, not mine, you deal with him!
- ✗ I do not want you to take my children to your parents' house!
- ✗ I forbid you from visiting your parents, they are simply evil!

These statements are simply cruel, selfish and immature. These can be construed as verbal and emotional abuse! The blessed Prophet warned us against such behaviour. He said, "To abuse one's parents is also a major sin." He was asked, "Can anyone abuse his parents?" "Yes," the Prophet replied, "If a person abuses someone else's parents and that person, in retaliation, abused the former's parents - then it is as though the former had abused his own parents."

Ask yourself this important question, "Am I forcing my spouse to be abusive towards his or her parents?" Naturally such a family life would be full of discord, misery and resentment. Bickering or giving ultimatums to your spouse to make a choice between marriage and family is not the solution.

Amongst the biggest sins in the eyes of Allah is to deliberately make ones parents cry because of cruel behaviour. A person asked the blessed Prophet, "Who has the greatest claim on me with regard to service and kind treatment?" The Prophet replied, "Your mother, and again your mother, and once again your mother. After hers, is the claim of your father, then that of your near relations, and then of the relations next to them." Yet the mother-in-law is too often vilified as the key to all the trouble. Even if the mother is hard to please, she is still the mother of your spouse.

Thus the obligation towards our mothers is three times higher than that towards our fathers. Of course, a father is entitled to his due share of love and affection. How can anyone ask a spouse to make a choice? Parents will always remain parents. We must give them love and affection no matter how difficult we find them.

"The pious son or daughter who casts a single look of affection at his/her parents receives a reward from God equal to the reward of an accepted Hajj," said the blessed Prophet. The people responded: "O blessed Prophet: if someone casts a hundred such glances of love and affection at his parents, what then?" The blessed Prophet observed, "Yes, indeed, even if one does so a hundred times a day, he will receive a hundred fold rewards. God is far greater than you imagine and is completely free from petty narrow-mindedness." *(Hadith Muslim)*

There are a small number of people in the community who use religious status as a justification to be cruel and dishonourable towards their in-laws or, in some cases, their parents. Some make statements such as "Your parents are non-Muslims" or "My parents are not believers". Is that fact that parents or in-laws are non-Muslim justification for rotten behaviour?

Asma, the daughter of Abu Bakr Al- Siddiq, said, "My mother came to Medina from Mecca to see me while she was still an unbeliever. She had come to demand something from me. I inquired with the blessed Prophet, 'My mother has come to see me and she is expecting something from me. May I oblige her?' He said: 'Yes, be kind to your mother.'" *(Hadith Bukhari and Muslim)*

Ibn 'Abbas reports that the blessed Prophet said, "The man who wakes up in the morning having previously discharged all the duties and obligations laid upon him by God concerning his parents, will find the two gates of Paradise open for him; and in case there is only one parent, the person will find one door of Paradise open for him. In contrast, if a man wakes up in the morning having previously disregarded any obligations or duties laid upon him by God concerning his parents, then he will find the two gates of Hell open for him; and in case one of the parents is alive, then the man will find one gate of Hell open for him." The man responded: "O blessed Prophet of God, if the parents are treating him wrongly, what then?" The blessed Prophet affirmed: "Yes, even if they are treating him wrongly; yes, indeed, even if they are treating him wrongly." *(Hadith Mishkat)*

Tips and tabs

Ten tips for better relationship with your in- laws

i. **Work with your spouse:** In-laws are often the focus of blame and reproach in marital disputes. Remember your spouse's parents have known him/her from the day he or she was conceived and loved them since the beginning. Never put him/her in the impossible position of having to make a choice by giving him/her an ultimatum such as "It's me or them". You are married to each other and in it together. The sooner you accept this, the sooner you will be motivated to work with your spouse to deal with problems. There is a long history of family bonds that no one should have to break. You can help and become part of the family; work with your spouse to solve problems.

ii. **Set ground rules and enforce them:** Happy families are not just close families all living under one roof and eating from the same pot. Keeping and balancing ties inevitably requires setting clear ground-rules. With your spouse, decide what's important and what's not. Sit with your in- laws and agree a set of mutually acceptable boundaries. If you do not want your in-laws to give your child fizzy drinks, then make it clear to them. If you would like your in-laws to not just barge into your house, but phone before coming, make sure you add that as a clause in your ground rules.

iii. **Know your limits:** In-laws may have expectations of what you should be, but that may not be who you are. Don't try to remake yourself into the person your in-laws want. Let me share with you the kind of expectations of a wife that some in-laws may dream of for their son – that she will be a wife, a cook, a cleaner, a housekeeper, a laundry lady, a nurse, a maid, a mother, a teacher, as well as being extremely devout and always with high level of faith and practice! Is it possible for one person to deliver so many roles effectively and live up to such high expectations? Make it clear that you are willing to work and get stuck in, but others need to do their fair share too. You have the full right to say no, but say it politely and firmly. Islam does not want you to be a door mat.

iv. **Communicate directly:** "Religion is sincerity" and "Religion is being straightforward and upright" exclaimed the blessed Prophet. Whenever possible avoid communicating through a third party. Don't ask your spouse to talk to his/her sibling about something s/he did that hurt your feelings. Sometime communicating through someone else can also be a form of backbiting, creating more rifts and spreading discord. Talk to him/her directly. If something bothers you, address it as soon as possible. Sometimes it's a genuine problem; other times, it might be a misunderstanding.

v. **Resolve conflicts:** Pushing all the problems under the carpet may seem attractive but experience tells us that if the problem is not resolved, if the conflict is not settled, it always comes back causing further trouble and heartache for all parties. You do not need every problem to be aired on the public lawn of your in-laws.

Do not keep running back to your parents with even your smallest quarrels. This would reduce your esteem in the eyes of your parents for they will lose confidence in your ability to solve problems and it will also increase their interference in your immediate family issues.

Let respective parties settle their own disputes. But any problems arising from the various and sometimes opposing interests and complex relationships are best resolved immediately.

vi. **Keep your nose out of other people's business:** If your mother-in-law has a problem with her husband, let them deal with it. Don't interfere. Don't tell your spouse how to improve their relationship with his/her parents. Do not get involved in your spouse's external family disputes unless your advice is asked for. The believer leaves alone things that does not concern him, advised the blessed Prophet. Never divulge family secrets!

vii. **Learn to control your temper and your mouth:** The worst time to discuss or resolve issues is when you are angry. Those who cannot control their tongue should always wait until they are calm and composed. A bit of time between anger and resolution is extremely healthy. Time heals many wounds and wounds many heal. While you are in the middle of an argument, be pleasant and polite. Spare your in-laws the insults and character attacks.

viii. **Be wise and mature:** Your parents will always love you, they have no choice, and it is in their genes. But your in-laws do not have to love you. Respecting in-laws is essential but do not expect your in-laws to have unconditional love for you. Accept the fact that your in-laws aren't your parents. To make this work, give in on small points and negotiate the key issues. Learn to see the situation from your in-laws' point of view. And even if you don't agree, be as the bigger person. Wisdom requires us to know where to draw the line. It is not wise to compare your wife to your mother or your husband to your dad. It could land you into a lot of trouble.

ix. **Be compassionate and respectful:** If you cannot be polite, if you cannot be nice and cannot express adequately, it is better for you to keep silent. Pretend to be nice, make up something kind to say and smile! Always treat your in-laws with compassion, respect and mercy. Maintain the good Islamic etiquettes with your sisters- and brothers-in-law. One of the most powerful signs of showing respect to your in-laws is to never forbid your wife or husband from visiting their parents. Give grandparents easy and reasonable access to their grandchildren.

x. **Keep your sense of humour:** In-laws-related jokes often go down well in public events. It is highly unlikely that these events are attended by your in-laws. It is important to keep a good sense of humour between you and your in-laws but check if your jokes are being taken as jokes or are causing serious offense.

You and your spouse are responsible for your family. You are more powerful than you think. You decide who and when people can visit you, when you take your holiday, how you celebrate Eid or birthdays, what food your children eat or what clothes they wear and access to them. No one can push you around unless you let them. In-laws do not need to be out-laws.

Checklist: Please place a tick if you agree or cross if you disagree

	Yes	No
I am happy to spend time with my spouse's family		
I look at my in-laws and I compare them to my own parents		
I consider my in-laws an addition to my family life		
I have no problem with my spouse spending time with his/her family		
I would be happy to live with my in-laws		
I would never make my spouse choose me over his/her family		

If you have-
less than Yes: Your relationship with your in-laws isin trouble
3-4 Yes: Your relationship needs fine tuning
5-6 Yes: You have done a good job with your relationship

Exercise 1:

SWOT analysis - Take a piece of A4 size paper. Draw a line in the middle of the page vertically and another horizontally. You should have four boxes. Label each box with the following headings: Strengths, Weaknesses, Opportunities and Threats. List under each of these headings all aspects of your relationship with your in-laws that are best described under these categories. Now choose the right moment and share it with your in-laws.

Creating a Muslim family is not just about me, it is about nurturing relationship and fostering support

How do I get married?

"Four things are from the traditions of the Prophets: modesty, applying perfume, using toothbrush and marriage"
(Hadith Tirmidhi)

I assume you have read the entire book by now. I hope you have had an enjoyable read so far and you feel ready to get married. So how do you go about finding a partner?

There are many ways you can find a potential spouse:

- Be introduced by your friends or family
- Meet at work, education, social or leisure space
- Meet through a match making agency
- Reply to a advert on the internet
- Meet at a mosque or study circle

In searching for a suitable spouse, the above means do not contradict Islam as long as you do not break the two following cardinal rules:

- **Never meet in secret** or at a place that is totally private. Private space in Islam is a space that is shut away from the public eye or a place where you could get up to mischief without getting caught. For example, the back of the cinema, inside your car which is parked at a private or isolated location or in the woods, beach, mountain, etc.

- **Never become physically involved**, i.e. sexually or indulge in activities which could lead to sex - for example, sexually-charged or erotic conversations; touching and caressing; or engaging in cyber-sex through emails, text messages or instant messengers.

Now that you have met someone, you should:

- Take references about the person from people who know them
- Speak to each other's parents and seek their blessing
- Objectively think through the issues including compatibility.

All of us come from a family; we are the way we are because of our family and our upbringing. Therefore, it is a very good idea to check the family background. A good knowledge of the family would also help you understand your prospective spouse better.

If you feel happy with everything, what do you do next?

- You could take the big step and formally propose either directly to the person or to the parents.
- Send a proposal using a 3rd party well-wisher.

Once your proposal has been accepted and parents have given their blessing, things are easy. Marriage in Islam is not a burden. It is a five-step process and can be done fairly quickly. The following is a quick summary of what should happen:

1. **Formal proposal and acceptance:** The individuals concerned, i.e. the couple, have agreed to the terms and conditions of the marriage proposal. This information is made known to the public or in some cultures they are announced as being 'engaged'.

2. **Engagement:** Although this is not necessary, many cultures have it. It should be made formal so that the couple can meet and talk freely, get to know each other and have the opportunity to make informed decisions. The golden rule in engagement is that nothing physical or sexual is allowed. The idea is that, without consummating the relationship, the period of courtship can lead to consolidated decision. At the end of it all the choices are clear: break the engagement or consummate the relationship.

3. **Mahr:** It is always given by the husband to his prospective wife before the marriage is consummated. Some consider it a gift or a mark of commitment to the marriage contract. The amount or the nature of the gift should be negotiated between the couple. There is a terrible practice in some communities where large sums of money are demanded by the wife's family, often leaving the prospective husband in debt. On the other hand there are people, who give less than their means, i.e. the amount is too low, and this does not demonstrate seriousness to the marriage contract. Some scholars have suggested one year's normal upkeep should be used as a bench mark when negotiating mahr.

The wife keeps this gift and would only return it if she initiated a divorce. The husband must not demand it back or withhold giving it. He should not ask her and certainly never demand from her a waiver from giving the Mahr. No family or husband should ever demand the wife to give the husband or his family any wedding gifts. Such demand or expectation is completely against the teachings of Islam.

4. **Solemnise the marriage:** The marriage must be legalised so that in case of problems, the legal process can facilitate a fair outcome. In countries where Nikah is not accepted as a legal contract, it is mandatory that Muslim couples register their marriage using local legal procedures. An imam usually performs the Nikah and issues a Nikah certificate. As part of the process he will confirm your details, ask if you accept each other as husband and wife in Islam, announce your mahr and deliver a brief sermon as a reminder of what is to be expected in marriage, as well as wishing you a happy marriage. The sermon must be given in the local language so people can understand it.

5. **Public declaration:** In Islam, marriage should never be kept a secret. The ceremony to celebrate the wedding is called "walima". The responsibility of organising the walima is usually the bridegroom's. However, there is no reason why the cost should not be shared by the bride and the groom and their families. The event should be a fun and happy occasion, balanced between cultural and celebratory expressions and the moral framework that Islam promotes.

You may go off to a honeymoon or stay at home. The choice is yours. Islam does not place any restrictions on what you can do to mark the beginning of the most important journey of your life. Whatever you do, be mindful of Allah who is aware of all our actions.

The blessed Prophet is reported to have said that **every religion has a distinctive feature and the distinctive feature of Islam is modesty.** Wedding arrangements including a wedding dress, walima arrangements, hired cars, cultural expressions and the honeymoon should not be an opportunity to show off or be extravagant. Allah hates those who are arrogant and wasteful. All things in moderation are also pleasing to the contented heart and most importantly Allah.

> Wedding is not a burden; it is an opportunity to celebrate the coming together of two people and two families.

Conclusion

The Prophet (peace be upon him) said to me, "O A'isha, be gentle, for gentleness has never been used in anything without beautifying it; and it has never been removed from something with out debasing it." *(Hadith Abu Dawood)*

The marriage contract gives a license to build a family and develop the partnership between a man and a woman according to Islam. It gives license to enjoy sex in the conjugal relationship. This is the only contract you would ever sign without anyone really checking your qualifications or credentials. Most of us don't know how to be married. Of course it is perfectly valid to learn all about it while you are on the actual journey; you learn together with your spouse.

But it would be ideal if you prepared for it. Take a marriage preparation course or simply read books on it. Ensure the course you take or the books that you read are written by reputable and qualified people.

In your mind, be clear about what you want from the marriage and what you are offering. In many cases, couples who have a clear idea of each other's expectations before they sign the contract lead a very fulfilling marital life.

Respecting and honouring your spouse means accepting that your spouse is also a human being, has needs, dreams, aspirations, feelings and emotions. We all have ambitions; so do our spouses. Understand that your spouse will forget, make mistakes and even get angry sometimes for good reasons and sometimes for no reason.

Fulfil your side of the contract; play your part to the best of your ability. Marriage is about working together and supporting your spouse in filling the gaps in the partnership.

Some people think that once they have the marriage certificate there is very little left to do! Appreciating each other forms the cornerstone of a successful marriage. Don't take each other for granted. Show each other how you still love each other and how aging together is only serving to deepen your feelings for each other.

If I was asked to sum up marriage in three words, describing the most important ingredients for a lasting marriage they would be honesty, compassion and patience.

I have tried my best to put together my thoughts to inspire you to find love, and to love someone special. I have attempted to share with you my personal thoughts and given you tips and suggestions. Anything good is from God and I thank him for it. Any mistakes are mine and I ask you in advance to forgive me.

I am always inspired by people who put words together which encompass all we want to say. Here are two final thoughts:

"What greater thing is there for two human souls than to feel that they are joined together to strengthen each other in all labour, to minister to each other in all sorrow, to share with each other in all gladness, to be one with each other in the silent unspoken memories?"
- George Eliot

"Let there be spaces in your togetherness."
- Kahlil Gibran